A Chinese
Garden of Serenity

Epigrams from the Ming Dynasty
'Discourses on Vegetable Roots'

'Only those who can appreciate
the least palatable of vegetable roots
know the meaning of life.'

Translated by Chao Tze-chiang

THE PETER PAUPER PRESS
Mount Vernon · New York

A CHINESE GARDEN OF SERENITY
written by Hung Tzu-ch'eng of
the Ming Dynasty, is a synthesis
of important ideas of Zen Buddhism, Taoism and Confucianism.
The author's own philosophy was
based on Confucian idealism. In
a sense, this Chinese work can
perhaps be compared with
Pascal's *Pensées*.

.   .   .

Cultured Japanese are much given
to the perusal of this book, and
find in it much to help their moral
discipline and spiritual insight.
Even Japanese who are engrossed
in practical life are interested in it.
Chao Tze-chiang has done well
in rendering these epigrams
into English.

.   .   .

DAISETZ TEITARO SUZUKI

‪ℐ‬NTRODUCTION

T HE *Discourses on Vegetable Roots* (Ts'ai Ken
T'an) is a synthesis of some ideas of Buddhism,
Taoism, and Confucianism, expressed in poetic
epigrams for the pleasure and instruction of
those who seek serenity.

The book was written by Hung Tzu-ch'eng,
also known as Hung Ying-ming. About Hung's
life we know very little. We do know that he
was alive in 1596, but when he was born and
when he died cannot be ascertained. According
to a preface to the *Discourses*, he lived in Shun-
tu County, Szechuan Province. As a young
man he led a dissipated life, but became a Zen
Buddhist monk in middle age. He was a good
friend of Yuan Liu-fen, the great historian, and
of Yu K'ung-chien, a prominent figure in the
political controversy of 1593. He left us five
books in addition to the present one.

The *Discourses on Vegetable Roots* must
have held strong interest for Chinese scholars,
because three of them wrote books after the
style and way of thinking of Hung Tzu-ch'eng.
These three books are the *Sweeping with a
Sword* by Lu Shao-heng of the Ming dynasty,
*A Continuation to the Discourses on Vegetable
Roots* by Shih Hsing-chai of the Ch'ing dynasty,

and the *Discourses on Vegetable Roots for My Family* by Liu Tzu-tsai, also of the Ch'ing dynasty.

The Chinese meaning of "vegetable roots" in the title is derived from a famous saying of Wang Hsin-min, a scholar of the Sung dynasty. He says that only those who can appreciate the least palatable of vegetable roots know the meaning of life. The tenor of the book is thus indicated in its title: simple, homely symbols of spiritual truths, as they have come to an unpretentious man.

In this book, Hung consciously strove to clothe his philosophical thought in antithetical aphorisms, and in that style few Chinese writers have succeeded so well. Almost all his abstract ideas are illustrated by concrete images, and his parallel sentences approximate the structure of a Chinese lü, or "tonally regulated" poem. Therefore my attempt in this rendering has been to recapture the stylistic beauty of the original in antithesis and parallelism so highly characteristic of the Chinese classical language.

I have undertaken this selected translation because it contains three types of philosophy which, I hope, may help ease some of the psychological tensions and conflicts in the West.

CHAO TZE-CHIANG

ᴀ GARDEN OF SERENITY

MOST people can read a book with words but not one without words, and they can play a lyre with strings but not one without strings. How can they derive tranquil pleasure from a book or a lyre, when they exercise their intelligence only on the material, but not on the spiritual, aspect of things?

IN EVERY human heart, there is a Book of Truth, bound with worn-out strings and torn bamboo-papers. In every human heart, there is also a Symphony of Nature, drowned out by sensual song and voluptuous dance. A man must sweep away all externals and search his inner being in order to experience joy.

WHEN the wind blows through the scattered bamboos, they do not hold its sound after it has gone. When the wild geese fly over a cold lake, it does not retain their shadows after they have passed. So the mind of the superior man begins to work only when an event occurs; and it becomes a void again when the matter ends.

A FEW fluttering green leaves and fallen red flowers on the doorstep, if they are gathered together, become the subject-matter of poetry. A mass of floating cloud and a sweep of glimmering mist before the window, if their meaning is apprehended, suggest a clue to the wisdom of Ch'anism.[1]

[1] The Chinese term for Zen Buddhism.

8

SINCE mountains, rivers, and the whole earth are but dust, what do you expect from the tiniest dust within dust? Since the flesh, the blood, and the entire human body are but a shadow, what do you look for in a shadow cast by another shadow? Thus, without wisdom one cannot have an enlightened mind.

IF A man could make his body spirit and appear in the shadow of cloud and mist, he would begin to apprehend that the common clay is a shackle. And if he could hear the tender voice of his inner self in the chirping of birds, he would be able to perceive that passions are spears.

NATURAL scenery — such as the azure mists on the hills, the ripples on the water, the shadow of a cloud on a pond, the hazy gleams among the grass, the expressions of blossoms under the moon, or the graceful manners of willows in the wind, all of which are existent and yet non-existent, half real and half unreal — is most agreeable to the human heart and most inspiring to the human soul. Such vistas are the wonder of wonders in the universe.

A MAN must neither be found by the Dharma[2] nor entangled by the Void in order to put his body and mind at ease.

[2] The Cosmic Law.

MANURE-WORMS are dirty, and yet they transform themselves into cicadas, which drink dew in the autumnal wind. Decayed grasses are not bright, and yet they give birth to glow-worms, whose luster matches the summer moon. Hence we know that cleanliness often comes from filth and brilliance from gloom.

* HEARKENING to the pealing of a bell on a silent night, one may be awakened from a dream of dreams. Gazing at the reflection of the moon on a transparent pool, one may visualize a spiritual body in one's physical body.

AFTER the ground has been swept, dust-clouds roll over it. When one begins to act, obstacles arise. After the pool has been dug, the moon shines on it. When one makes one's mind void, illumination is begotten.

STRAYING from Enlightenment, a man finds a happy land to be a sea of suffering, as water is frozen into ice; but awakening to Enlightenment, he discovers a sea of suffering to be a happy land, as ice is melted into water. Hence, we know that suffering and happiness are not two different moods and that straying from, and awakening to, Enlightenment are not two different frames of mind.

IF THE mind is as void as the interior of a bamboo, let us ask where is right or wrong. If the face of a man is as slender as a pine, we know that his gladness and grief cannot be revealed even in his eyebrows.

SINCE the Void is not void, a fond illusion of life is not true, and a bitter disillusionment of life is also not true. Let us ask Shakyamuni[3] what to do. Since to live in the world is to retreat from the world, an indulgence in desires is a suffering, and a suppression of desires is also a suffering. So we must in good faith hold to our integrity.

[3] Another name of Buddha.

THE MIND is like a bright pearl. If obstructed by material desires, it is like a pearl covered with mud and sand. But if clasped by passions, it is like a pearl adorned with silver and gold. Accordingly, a scholar is afraid not of an unclean malady, but of the difficult cure of a clean malady; and he fears not a barrier in events, but the difficult removal of a barrier in principles.

WHEN a man, with a jar of wine beside him, takes the heavens as a tent and the earth as a mat, he is in harmony with the life-giving forces. Who can say that inebriety is not a way to practice Ch'anist meditation?

To CONCUR with a web of circumstances is to dismiss it, and is like the harmony between flitting butterflies and fluttering flowers. To accord with an event is to nullify it, and is like the perfection of the full moon as round as a basin of water.

ACTORS paint their faces with powder and rouge in order to imitate Beauty or Ugliness. Where is their beauty or ugliness, after their songs are finished and the audience gone away? Chess-players contend avidly with each other in their moves in order to determine who will be the victor and who the vanquished. Where is their victory or defeat, after the game is over and the pieces are wrapped up?

AN AILMENT of the liver may cause blindness; a sickness of the kidney may result in deafness. Illness originates from the invisible, but, when showing a symptom, is bound to be visible. Therefore, the superior man, in order not to offend the Obvious, does not offend the Obscure.

LIFE'S fortune and misfortune are caused entirely by the mind. Shakyamuni said: "A burning desire for gain is a pit of fire, and an indulgence in greed is a sea of suffering. Once our mind is purified, a flame is turned into a pool; and once our mind awakens us from a dream of worldliness, our ship of life is anchored along the shore of the Great Beyond." Hence, a slight change of the mind can suddenly make a different situation. Should we not be careful?

HUMAN affairs are like a chess-game: only those who do not take it seriously can be called good players. Life is like an earthen pot: only when it is shattered, does it manifest its emptiness.

A PIGEON, when annoyed by the bells on its neck, will fly higher and higher, but it does not know that to fold its wings will stop the tinkling of the bells. A man, when irked by his shadow, may run faster and faster, but he does not understand that to stay in a shady place will eliminate his shadow. So the foolish people who run fast and fly high find a smooth ground to be a sea of suffering, whereas people of insight who stay in the shade and fold their wings discover a craggy slope to be a level road.

HEARKENING to the crying cranes under a frosty firmament or the crowing cocks on a snowy night, one can catch the pure spirit of heaven and earth. Beholding the flying birds in the clear sky or the playful fishes in the flowing water, one can understand the life-force in the universe.

SITTING by a teapoy in a room bathed with pure breezes and moonbeams, one can read the mind of Heaven in every thing. Walking along a running brook in the clouded mountain, one can observe the mysteries of the Tao[4] in every moment.

[4] The Cosmic Process or the Way.

LOOKING at the busy bees in a fragrant and luxuriant garden, one may become disillusioned about the life of the senses and the ways of the world. Beholding the sleeping swallows in a quiet and humble hovel, one may arouse in oneself a cool pleasure and a deep contemplation.

WHEN a man leisurely looks at the flies hurtling against a paper-screen, he may scornfully laugh at those idiots who make obstacles for themselves. When he quietly watches the jackdaws squabbling for a nest, he may sigh with regret for those eminent men who struggle with vain heroism.

WHILE soaring in the sky and over the earth, a roc felt that its journey was narrow and short. While perching on an old pine, shrouded by a cloud, a crane knows that its dream is serene and leisurely.

A BEAUTIFUL lady who does not care for rouge is like the sparsely-poised plum blossoms illuminated by pallid moonlight. A devotee of Ch'anism who does not indulge in emptiness is like a green lotus blooming upon a bluish pond.

SUDDENLY gazing at the colorful clouds above the horizon, one wonders if all good things are not inane. Often-times beholding the idle trees in the mountains, one believes that a man of leisure is happy.

WHEN a bird is frightened out of its wits or a flower splashes its tear-drops, they both embrace ardor and zeal. How can they calmly appreciate the chilly wind or the gelid moon?

WHEN a man has realized the essential nature of his mind, he can speak of enlightening his mind. And when he has exhausted the ordinary ways of the world, he is able to discourse on his seclusion from the world.

THOSE who prefer quietude to noise retreat from people into solitude, but they do not know that to be alone is a self-obsession and to aim at quiescence is the root of action.

AS THERE is the clear sky with the bright moon, whither can moths not fly? But they dash only into night candles. As there are clear fountains and green bamboos, what can barn-owls not drink and peck? But they are fond of putrid rats. Alas, are not many people in the world like moths and barn-owls?

BOILING tea and hearkening to the singing of the kettle, one can understand the principles of yin and yang[5] by watching the fire inside the stove. Strolling under catalpa trees and stopping to see a game of chess, one can apprehend the motives of life and death from the moving of the pieces.

[5] Yin means darkness, femininity or passivity. Yang means light, masculinity, or activity.

22

WHILE a crane is standing among chickens, it may be said to be incomparably preëminent. But if it looks at a roc flying over the wide sea, it finds itself dwarfed. Moreover, if it gazes at a phoenix soaring towards the zenith, it feels itself infinitely smaller.

THOSE desolate door-steps where foxes crouch and those deserted terraces where rabbits ramble, might in olden days have been places for singing and dancing. There where yellow flowers are chilled by dew and where faded grass is obscured by mist, might once have been battlegrounds. Can prosperity and decline remain constant? Where are the victors and the vanquished of old?

23

WHEN a man, in exhilaration, lies intoxicated on strewn flowers, the heavens become his blanket and the earth his pillow. And when he, in subduing artifice, sits in a trance on a huge rock, he feels that from time immemorial to the present moment all things are but ephemeral.

FISHING is a pleasure of retirement, yet the angler has the power to let the fish live or die. Chess-playing is an enjoyable pastime, yet the players are motivated by the idea of war.

AS THE chimpanzee bleeds over a cup, we deride its fondness for wine. As the martin nests above a curtain, we pity its love for indolence.

WHEN a man contends for supremacy, he contends like the sparks flashed between two stones. How long can those sparks last? When he fights for victory, he fights in the horn of a snail. How large a world is that horn?

IF A man aims at finding the ebb and flow of life in a decayed tree or withered grass, an inaudible sound or a savorless taste, he becomes a bellows for the fires of heaven and earth and a root to men and to objects.

EVEN if a man has clenched the past and the present in his two fists, he has finally to release them. And if he has shouldered the wind and the moon with a bamboo-cane, he has eventually to unload them.

25

WHEN birds twitter to one another, their pleasure is mutual; when a flower grows on a twig, its fragrance can rise perpetually. Here we find the spirit of unity of one thing with another. When the view in a field is not interrupted even by a hillock, or when the light of the sky meets the water of the sea, there is the state of pervasion from above and below.

FLOWERS display their beauty to the bright spring. But when they are pounded by a downpour of rain and a gust of wind, they are hastened back to dust. Bamboos persist in the integrity of their elegance. Even though they are beaten by frost one morning and snow another, they remain true to their green jade hue.

A MIGHTY man may give away a thousand chariots for fame; a greedy man may fight for a copper coin. Here we see a difference between personalities as great as the separation between a star and an abyss. But the love for good repute is like the love for profit. A monarch may map out plans for his country; a beggar may cry for a meal. Here we find a distinction between positions as clear as the distance between the sky and the earth. But is painful thinking dissimilar from bitter wailing?

BY THE side of Honor, Humiliation waits. When honored, one ought not be high-spirited. Behind Poverty, Prosperity follows. When impoverished, why should one be low-spirited?

FROM the conventional viewpoint, all things, events, and human relationships are variable; but from the standpoint of the Tao, all of them are constant. Why should one bother to differentiate? Why need one take or give?

A MIND full of light is like a blue sky found in a somber room, but an intention tainted with darkness is like the Demons discovered under the white sun.

IF I gain by my use of objects, I am not glad; and if I lose, I am not sad. For the good earth amply provides transcendental bliss. If I overcome my enslavements by objects, I am hated; and if I accord with them, I am loved. So love and hatred, even in the slightest degree, produce bondage.

INSECTS in the autumn, like birds in the spring, cherish their nature. Why should one thoughtlessly be happy or sad? Old trees, like new flowers, sustain their vitality. Why should one recklessly distinguish between beauty and ugliness?

THE LARGER the fortune hoarded, the greater the loss. The higher the climb, the quicker the fall.

THE ATTITUDE of people towards me may be warm or cold, but I respond neither gladly nor resentfully; the tastes of the world may be savory or insipid, but I react neither happily nor disgustedly. If one does not fall into the trap of the mundane, one knows the ways of living in, and escaping from, the world.

29

ALTHOUGH the teeth are gone, the tongue still remains. Hence the strong does not eventually triumph over the weak. Although the door decays, its hinges are not ruined by termites. Can the rigid be better than the flexible?

SINCE there are rolling billows in the East Sea, one need not be wrought up about mundane things. Since there is no spare space in the cemetery of the North Hill, one need not be gloomy about life.

THAT happiness endures which comes from the grinding together of anguish and ecstasy, and from the intensity of the grinding. That knowledge is true which comes from searching into doubts and beliefs, and from the depth of the searching.

30

EVEN if a phoenix is roasted and a dragon boiled for food, after the chopsticks are put down, their savors are not different from those of pickled vegetables. Even if gold and jade are hung for adornments, after they have been burned to ashes, they are not other than potsherds.

WHILE drinking wine, get not fuddled. While admiring flowers, see them not in full bloom.

WHEN a man lies in eight feet of space at night and eats two catties[6] of rice each day, why need he concern himself in any way? When he has read a large collection of books and is endowed with great talents, he may not have leisure even for one day.

[6] A catty equals one and one-third pounds.

WHETHER in favor or in humiliation, be not dismayed. Let your eyes leisurely look at the flowers blooming and falling in your courtyard. Whether you leave or retain your position, take no care. Let your mind wander with the clouds folding and unfolding beyond the horizon.

A TASTE derived from tranquility and ease is dilute, but lasts longer.

TO BOAST of fame is not such a pleasure as to avoid it; to be versed in worldly affairs does not bring such leisure as to be unconcerned with them. Lo, a lone cloud idling across a mountain peak does not care whether it stays there or passes on; while the bright moon hanging in the firmament is indifferent as to whether the world is silent or noisy.

To GET rid of scoundrels and sycophants one must leave them an outlet. If they are denied even a foothold, it is like closing the ways of escape at rat-holes so the rats must gnaw all the good things inside.

GLORY and ignominy come from the same stem. Why should one crave glory, if one detests ignominy? Life and Death are of the same root. Why should one dread death, if one clings to life?

WHEN the fisherman's net is spread, a swan may be caught in it; when a grass-hopper is greedy, a sparrow may take advantage of it from behind. Here is one intrigue against another and one change against another. How can ingenuity be dependable?

A MAN can apprehend Truth at another's intimation, but he will stray from it. Hence that is not so enlightening as apprehending it completely by himself. And he can secure a pleasure from an extraneous source, but he will lose it. Therefore that is less secure than an ecstasy from within.

TO BE circumspect makes one's spirit hard pressed; to be carefree makes one's mind innocent. Do these apply only to the elegance and crudity of poetry and prose? I often see that a wary man acts with artifice, while an unrestrained man reveals his true nature. There, too, we have a distinction between the life and the death of the human heart.

WHEN the mind is possessed of Reality, it feels tranquil and joyous even without music or song, and it produces a pure fragrance even without incense or tea.

WHEN a man of insight appreciates the music of a lyre, calligraphy, poetry, or painting, he nurtures his mind with them; but a worldly man delights only in their physical appeals. When a noble-minded man appreciates mountains, rivers, clouds, or other natural objects, he develops his wisdom with them; but a vulgar man finds pleasure only in their apparent splendor. So we know that things have no fixed attribute. Whether they are noble or ignoble depends upon one's understanding.

To APPRECIATE one does not need to look afar; to be inspired one does not need to have much. In a little jagged stone or small basin, a man may visualize the grandeur of mountains or rivers ten thousand miles long; in a word or sentence of the ancient sages or worthies, he may read their minds. If so, he has the vision of the noble and the mind of the wise.

THE GREEN bamboo, withstanding frigid frost, appreciates its integrity, yet its self-appreciation does not spoil its elegance. The crimson lotus, dallying with autumnal water, is gorgeous in its color, yet its gorgeousness does not injure its purity.

THE RADIANT sun and the blue heaven may suddenly be blotted out by claps of thunder and strokes of lightning; a sweeping windstorm and a furious tempest may quickly end with a resplendent moon and a clear sky. How, then, can the Ether be in the least coagulated or the Great Void be in the least obstructed? The human mind should be of this nature.

A DROP of water has the tastes of the water of the seven seas: there is no need to experience all the ways of worldly life. The reflections of the moon on one thousand rivers are from the same moon: the mind must be full of light.

BEFORE the wild goose flies near, you have drawn your bow; and after the rabbit has fled, you call for an arrow. You take no advantage of an opportunity. When the gale stops, the waves no longer surge; and when the boat lies at anchor, the passengers disembark. They know the secret of ending an event.

WHEN a man's mind is as limpid as if it were a burnished mirror or a still pond, there is under the heavens nothing detestable. And when his temper is as serene as if he were under the beautiful sun and in the light breezes, there is on the earth no one hideous.

A CONVENTIONAL man delights in his prosperity, but the superior man's happiness comes from his adversity. A conventional man grieves at his dissatisfaction, but the superior man's sorrow arises from his satisfaction. This is so because the sorrow and happiness of a conventional man are induced by passion and those of the superior man by intellect.

WHETHER time is long or short, and whether space is broad or narrow, depend upon the mind. Those whose minds are at leisure can feel one day as long as a millennium, and those whose thought is expansive can perceive a small house to be as spacious as the universe.

WHEN there is no commotion and agitation in a man's mind, he finds every place as peaceful as a verdant hill or a green tree. When there are transforming and nurturing powers in his nature, he discovers every thing as lively as a leaping fish or a flying hawk.

MAN CAN triumph over Heaven; a will, being concentrated, can move the spirit. Accordingly, the superior man cannot be moulded by Heaven.

MOUNTAINS and forests are scenes of wonder. Once they are frequented by people, they are debased into market-places. Calligraphy and paintings are things of beauty. Once they are craved by people, they are degraded into merchandise.

IF A man could clear the meanness from his face, his looks would show no ugliness. And if he could empty the worldliness from his heart, his language would bear high meanings.

THE SUPERIOR man speaks not of life, since to cherish the mind is to root oneself in life; nor speaks he of Heaven, because to augment human efforts can reverse Divine Providence.

THE PURPOSE of the superior man is as clear as the blue sky or as bright as the white sun; it must not be kept from being known. But the talent of the superior man is like the jade hidden in a rock or the pearl covered with a shell; it must not easily become known.

FEELINGS that are the common traits of mankind are called human nature. Without feelings, human nature cannot be observed. Desires that are just are termed Truth. Without desires, Truth cannot be understood. Accordingly, the superior man does not suppress his feelings but keeps them in repose, nor does he eradicate his desires but reduces them.

WHERE it is rancid and nasty, flies and mosquitoes crowd in to suck; where it is sweet and fragrant, bees and butterflies invade in swarms. Therefore the superior man neither undertakes a foul deed nor seeks to make a famous name. He keeps his pristine spirit and never displays his brilliance.

THOSE who express loathing for pomp and vainglory might, on encountering them, revel in them. Those who profess rejoicing at contentment and simplicity might, in experiencing them, become bored with them. So one must sweep away enthusiasm and indifference, eliminate predilection and aversion, forget pomp and vainglory, and delight in contentment and simplicity.

A SCHOLAR, when in political power, ought to be firm and just in his conduct, peaceful and easy in his temper. Never should he be so unscrupulous as to have traffic with an unsavory partisan, or so violent as to provoke a venomous scorpion.

HAVING observed human feelings, one begins to know the value of nonchalance and detachment. Having experienced the tastes of the world, one is able to learn the truthfulness of contentment and simplicity.

HUMAN feelings are frail; the ways of the world are rugged. When a man cannot go forward, he should know how to take a step backward; but when he can go on, he ought to have the grace of yielding a little.

WALKING along a narrow path, one should leave a margin; tasting rich delicacies, one should share a morsel. These are the happiest ways of dealing with the world.

WHEN flies attach themselves to the tail of a galloping horse, they move at high speed. But it is difficult for them to efface the shame of being an appendage. When vines entwine themselves around a tall pine, they reach an awesome height. But they cannot erase the disgrace of being a dependent.

CONTENTMENT should be tested in a world of vanity; calmness should be investigated in a place of turmoil.

THE SPIRIT of man communes with Heaven; the omnipotence of Heaven resides in man. Is the distance between Heaven and man very great?

IF I were a furnace or a smelting fire, why should I worry about my inability to refine crude gold and rusty iron? If I were a wide sea or a long river, why should I be concerned with my incapacity to admit tributary streamlets and muddy brooks?

LIFE is originally a puppet show. But when a man holds the handle and controls the strings without disorder, he can have the freedom of his expansion or contraction, and the command of his action and inaction. Thus, he is not manipulated but remains outside the theater of life.

TO WORK under difficulty is like rowing a boat against the wind. To learn through hardship is like obtaining gold by sifting sand.

To CONVERT a setback into a success should be like riding a horse at the edge of a precipice. Be not so careless as to whip it even once. To accomplish a task on the verge of completion should be like sailing a boat upstream in rapids. Be not so lazy as to stop paddling for even one stroke.

VIRTUE is the foundation of all achievements; no house whose foundation is not solid can be enduring. The mind is the root of all offshoots; no tree whose roots are rotten can be flourishing.

A SUSPICIOUS man, looking at the shadow of a bow in a cup, is frightened into mistaking it for a snake, and, hearing people speak in the market, believes a tiger is howling.

WHEN a man does not establish himself on a high plane, it is like brushing clothes in the dust or washing feet in the mud. How can he then be transcendent? And when he deals with the world without yielding a step, it is like a moth flying into a candle or a ram butting against a hedgerow. How can he then be happy?

PURITY can tolerate the unclean; benevolence can make sound judgments; cleverness does not pry so as to offend; straightness does not unbend what is crooked. These, like the unsweetness of the sweetened meat and the unsaltiness of the salted sea-delicacy, are said to be admirable virtues.

A GREEDY man may be materially rich, but spiritually poor; a contented man may be materially poor, but spiritually rich. One who holds a high position may feel physically at ease, but mentally fatigued; one who has a low position may feel physically fatigued, but mentally at ease. Which of these is a gain and which is a loss, which is real and which unreal, a man of insight can, of course, distinguish for himself.

VIRTUE is the master of talent; talent is the servant of virtue. If one has talent and no virtue, one is like a family without a patriarch in which a servant may act as he pleases. How then can there be no mischief like that of an elf?

IN SWEEPING winds and driving rains, birds feel melancholy; under the radiant sun and in the light breezes, grasses and trees flourish cheerfully. Hence we know that, even for one day, there should not be absence of harmony between the heavens and the earth or banishment of joy from the human heart.

TO BE conscientious is an admirable virtue, but to be painstaking does not tranquilize the mind or delight the heart. To be contented is noble, but to be lethargic does not enable one to benefit men or to utilize things.

BETWEEN right and wrong and between righteousness and iniquity, one ought not to make the least compromise, otherwise one will be at a loss to effect a fit acceptance or a proper rejection. Between an advantage and a disadvantage and between a gain and a loss, one ought not to make too precise a differentiation, otherwise one will be prone to egotistic pursuit or selfish avoidance.

TO CHECK the evils of the time within their drift is like the dispersing of summer heat by the gentle breezes. To mingle with the vulgar and yet retain decency is like the reflection upon the fleecy clouds of pallid moonlight.

LIFE abounds in filthy places; fish are rare in clear water. Therefore the superior man maintains his open-mindedness of containing the sordid and accepting the mean, and does not hold to the behavior of preferring the clean and shunning the vulgar.

IT IS not clever to pry; but to pry into what others cannot, is cleverness. It is not brave to insist on victory; but to overcome what others cannot, is bravery.

WARM weather fosters growth; cold weather destroys it. Thus a man with an unsympathetic temperament has scant joy; but a man with a warm and friendly heart has overflowing blessings, and his beneficence will extend to posterity.

ONE'S wickedness should not be kept in darkness; one's goodness should not be brought to light. Therefore wickedness, if exposed, is less harmful, but if hidden, more harmful; goodness, if shown, is less beneficial, but if concealed, more beneficial.

GREAT wickedness lurks in a soft spot: a wise man is alert against a needle inside the cotton. Deep hatred originates in love: a man of insight avoids the honey on the sharp point of a knife.

IF A man has done an evil act and is afraid lest it should become known, there is still a way of goodness in his evil. But if he has done a good deed and is eager that it be known, then even that good is a source of evil.

MANY think that they can become clear about things by prying; but clarity often turns out to be obscurity. So the superior man cultivates his wisdom with tranquility. Many also think that an accomplishment can be accelerated by vigor; but haste often causes delay. So the superior man tempers his levity with gravity.

A TRUE heart can cause snow to fly in a summer's day, a fortified city to fall, or a stone to be pierced; but a hypocrite has only his common clay without a spiritual master. When he is with others, his countenance is hideous; and, when alone, his body and his shadow are ashamed of each other.

How can the spending of thousands of gold coins to form acquaintance with eminent or influential people, be as good as pouring half the rice out of a gourd to relieve the hunger of the poor? How can the building of a stately edifice to attract more guests, be as good as repairing a thatched hut to shelter the humble and the neglected?

How can a tribute paid to the wealthy and powerful be as good as a eulogy received from the poor and humble? How can the visit of a friend from a distant land be as enjoyable as the confidence of a member of the family?

THOSE who depend upon the power of others are like the parasites on a tree: when the tree is chopped, the parasites are bereft of life. Those who covet wealth are like the worms in a human body: when the human body dies, the worms perish. With their power and wealth such persons at the beginning are pernicious to others and at the end ruin themselves. That is, indeed, the bane of power and wealth.

WHEN a man regards wealth and power as fleeting as a cloud, it is not necessary for him to be a recluse living in a cliff or grotto. When his fondness for natural scenery is not so deep-rooted as an incurable disease, he is as if intoxicated with wine and absorbed in poetry.

A YOUTH should perform every action with an earnest intent. If his intent is irresolute; he is as flippant as a duck flapping its wings on water. How can he ruffle up his pinions for flight into the empyrean? An elder should forget his affection for all his past deeds. If his affection becomes intense, he is as toilsome as a colt in harness. How can he liberate his body from the reins?

HEROIC deeds and magnificent plans are often initiated by leisurely and serene people, so one should not be over-occupied. Great prosperity and supreme blessedness are enjoyed mostly by munificent and bounteous families, therefore there is no need to be finicky.

ONCE a man is infected with avarice, he reduces his strength to weakness, turns his wisdom into folly, converts his benevolence into malice, and changes his cleanliness to squalor.

A MAN with a heart full of determination and perseverance can enjoy the myriad miracles of his mind.

IT REQUIRES a pure mind to read the classics and learn from the ancients. Otherwise, when a man happens to know a good deed of olden times, he may make use of it to serve his selfish ends; and when he hears a noble sentence from the classics, he may take advantage of it to conceal his shortcomings.

WHEN a man is wealthy and powerful, he should know the sufferings of the poor and humble. And when he is young and strong, he should think of the sore distress of old age.

THE SICKNESS of age was caused in youth; the vices of decadence originated in time of glory. Therefore the superior man particularly fears attaining fullness and reaching perfection.

IT IS easy to dodge the arrow of an enemy, but difficult to avoid the spear of a friend. It is also easy to escape from the pitfall of suffering, but difficult to get out of the snare of pleasure.

THERE is no need to worry that a youth will not be vigorous, but we are afraid lest his vigor might turn out to be rudeness. So impetuosity must be restrained. There is also no need to worry that an elder will not be sedate, but we fear lest his sedateness might prove retrograde. Therefore inertia must be discouraged.

WHEN a man is at peace, he ought to be as alert as if he were in trouble; so he can forestall an unforeseen contingency. And when he is in trouble, he ought to be as calm as if he were at peace; thus he can bring to an end his crisis.